cakes and
cookies

Written by Malcolm Long

imagine THAT!™

Imagine That! is an imprint of Top That! Publishing plc,
Tide Mill Way, Woodbridge, Suffolk, IP12 IAP, UK
www.topthatpublishing.com
Copyright © 2010 Top That! Publishing plc
Imagine That! is a trademark of Top That! Publishing plc.

Contents

Contents

The Joys of Baking

There is something magical and evocative of childhood about making cakes and cookies. However, very few commercially produced varieties, including even those that are very expensive, can match baking your own.

Home-baked cakes and cookies are very simple to make and many have a lightness that is irresistible, with a flavour that is only possible from something lifted from your own oven. The smells of baking are hard to beat — who doesn't relish the delicious aromas of ginger, golden syrup, the zest of orange or lemons and the smell of almonds, as they pervade your home.

Wise estate agents suggest roasting coffee prior to showing prospective clients around houses that are for sale, but a baking batch of cakes or cookies will definitely clinch the deal. Most of us have made them at some time, whether it was at school or on a rainy Saturday afternoon helping mum. Eating your home-made treats may well play havoc with your waistline, but baking them does wonders for stress and will make you very popular with friends and family.

This book includes a fantastic selection of traditional-style cakes and cookies, but also contains great new ideas for sweet treats that the whole family can enjoy: from bite-sized brownies to petit fours, meringues to sticky cereal delights and lots more that will really tantalise the taste buds.

Equipment

Baking cakes and cookies doesn't require an armada of tools and equipment, but you will need the essentials such as reliable kitchen scales, mixing bowls and a rolling pin. The following should also be noted to ensure your efforts run smoothly and achieve the best results.

Try to have several different sieves. Whenever possible, sieve flours and fine sugars, or anything which may develop lumps, prior to use.

Many of us won't have the luxury of a large kitchen, but aim to work tidily and give yourself the maximum space you can afford. Clear up as you go along. This will allow you to enjoy the fruits of your labour without being confronted with a sink full of washing-up.

Remember the basic rules of hygiene: wash your hands before starting and between handling different ingredients and stages. Many tasks are much better performed manually, but hands are just like any other kitchen tool and must be kept clean.

Try to keep some good sharp knives to work with. Blunt knives are dangerous as you have to apply too much pressure to cut with them, and slips are more likely to cause damage to misplaced fingers.

Always use a clean chopping board for cutting. Cutting directly onto work surfaces will scratch them and blunt your knives.

Choose large mixing bowls which may appear larger than necessary, but will allow you to beat or whisk without the ingredients being splashed around the kitchen. If you have the kitchen space, there are various kitchen gadgets you might find useful: including food processors, mixing machines, liquidisers or hand-held electric whisks — all of which can save you time and a lot of arm ache.

Cooking Tips

Ovens

If you are going to do a lot of baking then a large oven, preferably forced air or fan assisted is best, since these will allow food to brown evenly in all parts of the oven. With a conventional non-assisted oven, it is safer to use only the top two shelves and to keep baking trays at least 2–3 cm apart to allow heat to circulate. You will need to swap the trays around to ensure even cooking and browning. Try also to keep them away from the walls or door of the oven to avoid the food burning.

Baking sheets and trays

It is a good idea to buy the best baking sheets and trays you can afford. There are many varieties of non-stick trays to choose from and these are very useful and effective. However, heat-proof rubber matting and moulds are now widely available in many shapes and sizes; they are extremely easy to use and give great results. Although expensive, they are very effective when used in or out of the oven. A cheaper alternative is silicone paper which is reusable if not burnt and can be cut to any size quite easily. Whichever baking trays you choose, they should be flat with very low sides to allow the heat to travel evenly across the food being cooked.

Temperatures

The temperatures given in this book are approximate since no two ovens are ever the same. It is also true that however strictly you follow the recipe, the mixtures will always vary slightly.

Cooking times

To test if cakes are cooked, gently press the top. If they are firm to the touch then they should be done. To test whether cookies are done, first check the colour. Most are cooked when they have reached a pale, golden colour. Cool the cakes and cookies on wire racks before being stored. Biscuits which are to be rolled or shaped need to be formed before they cool; if they harden, a few seconds in a warm oven will soften them and allow for reshaping.

Storage

If biscuits are to be kept for any length of time they are better stored uncooked. This is done by shaping them in the usual way on a baking sheet but placing them in the freezer instead of in the oven. When the biscuits are set, remove from the baking sheets and store between layers of cling film in a plastic box in the freezer. Cooked biscuits and cakes should always be kept in an airtight container or tin.

Cakes

Victoria Sponge

Victoria Sponge

You will need:

- 100 g (4 oz) butter
- 100 g (4 oz) caster sugar
- 2 eggs
- 100 g (4 oz) self-raising flour
- 50 g (2 oz) strawberry jam
- 50 g (2 oz) whipped cream

Serves 12

1. Preheat the oven to 180°C / 350°F / gas mark 4.

2. Line the two cake tins with baking parchment.

3. Mix the butter and sugar together with an electric whisk. Next, add the eggs and continue to whisk.

4. Sift the flour into the mixture with a sieve and fold in using a spoon. The mixture should be light and creamy – if it isn't add a drop of milk.

5. Divide the mixture between the cake tins and gently spread out with a spatula.

6. Place the tins in a preheated oven for 20–25 minutes, or until the cakes are golden brown.

7. Add the jam and cream to the top of one cake, sandwich both cakes together, then serve!

Chocolate and Raspberry Cake

Chocolate and Raspberry Cake

You will need:
- 200 g (7 oz) butter
- 150 g (5 oz) sugar
- 3 free-range eggs
- 175 g (6 oz) self-raising flour
- 80 g (3 oz) unsweetened cocoa powder
- a few drops of vanilla essence
- 1 tbsp milk

For the filling:
- 450 g (1 lb) mascarpone
- 15 ml (½ fl.oz) milk
- 200 g (7 oz) chocolate
- 150 g (5 oz) sifted icing sugar
- 150 g (5 oz) raspberries

Serves 8–10

1. Preheat the oven to 180°C / 350°F / gas mark 4 and grease a 23 cm (9 in.) springform cake tin.

2. Cream together the butter and sugar and add the beaten eggs separately. Sift the flour and cocoa together and fold them into the egg mixture. Add a few drops of vanilla essence and the milk.

3. Transfer to the cake tin and bake in the centre of the oven for 35–40 minutes. Allow the cake to cool on a wire cooling rack.

4. Meanwhile, beat the mascarpone and milk to form a smooth cream.

5. Melt the chocolate in a heatproof bowl over a saucepan of barely simmering water. Allow the chocolate to cool a little and then add it to the mascarpone. Add sifted icing sugar and mix well. Refrigerate for 30 minutes.

6. Cut the cake in half and spread one-third of the chocolate mascarpone on one side. Place half of the raspberries on the filling and carefully replace the top half of the cake.

7. Use the rest of the mascarpone cream to decorate the top and sides of the cake. Finish with the remaining raspberries.

Gâteau St Honore

Gâteau St Honore

You will need:
- ½ small packet frozen puff pastry

For the choux pastry:
- 80 ml (3 fl.oz) water
- 25 g (1 oz) butter
- 15 g (½ oz) sugar
- 50 g (2 oz) strong flour
- 2 eggs

For the glaze:
- 100 g (4 oz) sugar

For the filling:
- 4–5 sponge fingers
- 2–3 tbsp brandy
- 200 ml (7 fl.oz) whipping cream
- 25 g (1 oz) caster sugar
- a few drops of vanilla essence
- 1 tbsp pistachio nuts, chopped

Serves 6–8

1. Roll out the puff pastry approx 3 mm (¼ in.) thick. Use a pastry ring or small plate to cut the pastry into a circle.

2. Lay the pastry on a sheet of silicone paper and allow to rest for an hour. Prick the base closely with a fork.

To make the choux pastry:

1. Boil the water in a pan and add the butter and sugar. When boiling, remove from the heat and stir in the flour.

2. Return to the heat and cook until the mixture comes clearly away from the sides of the pan. Remove and allow the mixture to cool. Beat in the eggs, a little at a time.

3. Take a piping bag and, using a medium star nozzle, pipe a single ring of choux pastry around the puff pastry. Pipe six separate choux buns on another baking sheet, and bake at 200°C / 400°F / gas mark 6 until crisp.

To make the glaze:

1. Boil the sugar with 2 tbsp water in a pan until the sugar starts to caramelise. Then, dip the base of the pan quickly into cold water.

To assemble:

1. Dip the bases of the choux buns into the melted sugar and stick them on the top of the choux ring.

2. Use a spoon to dribble melted sugar over the choux pastry edge and over the choux buns to give a decorative edge before the sugar sets.

3. Dice the sponge fingers and soak in the brandy. Then, scatter these onto the gâteau base.

4. Whip the cream with the sugar and vanilla and pipe or spoon over the diced sponge fingers to fill the gâteau.

5. Decorate with the pistachio nuts.

Chocolate and Pear Double-layer Cake

Chocolate and Pear Double-layer Cake

You will need:

- 175 g (6 oz) unsalted butter, softened
- 150 g (5 oz) light soft brown sugar
- 3 free-range eggs (at room temperature)
- 175 g (6 oz) self-raising flour
- 50 g (2 oz) cocoa powder
- 3–4 ripe pears, peeled, cored and sliced
- 40 g (1½ oz) light muscovado sugar
- 1 tsp cinnamon
- handful of pine nuts

Serves 8–10

1. Preheat the oven to 180°C / 350°F / gas mark 4 and grease and flour a 23 cm (9 in.) springform cake tin.

2. Cream together the butter and sugar until light and fluffy. Add the beaten eggs, one at a time, mixing well after each one has been added.

3. Sift the flour and cocoa powder together twice. Gradually fold the flour and cocoa into the creamed mixture, a few spoonfuls at a time.

4. Transfer half of the mixture to the tin and arrange a layer of pear slices over the top.

5. Mix the muscovado sugar and cinnamon, breaking up any lumps in the sugar, and sprinkle the pears with half of this. Spoon on the rest of the cake mixture and level it with a warm palette knife.

6. Place the remaining pears on top of the cake and sprinkle them with the sugar and cinnamon, and a handful of pine nuts.

7. Bake in the centre of the oven for 45–50 minutes.

White Chocolate and Lime Celebration Cake

White Chocolate and Lime Celebration Cake

You will need:
- 250 g (9 oz) unsalted butter
- 400 g (14 oz) caster sugar
- 5 free-range eggs
- 150 ml (5 fl.oz) sour cream
- 2 tsp amaretto almond liqueur
- 300 g (10 oz) plain flour
- 100 g (4 oz) unsweetened cocoa powder
- 50 g (2 oz) ground almonds
- 1 tsp baking powder
- ½ tsp bicarbonate of soda
- white and dark chocolate, to decorate

For the filling:
- 600 g (1 lb, 5 oz) mascarpone
- 50 ml (2 fl.oz) milk
- 175 g (6 oz) icing sugar, sifted
- grated zest and juice of two limes
- 80 g (3 oz) white chocolate, grated

Serves 14–16

1. Preheat the oven to 160°C / 325°F / gas mark 3 and grease and line a deep 25 cm (10 in.) cake tin with a removable base.

2. Cream the butter and sugar together until pale and fluffy. Add the beaten eggs, one at a time, mixing well, then add the sour cream and amaretto.

3. Sift the flour, cocoa powder, ground almonds, baking powder and bicarbonate of soda twice, holding the sieve up high to allow as much air into the ingredients as possible. Fold them into the cake mixture gently.

4. Transfer the mixture to the cake tin and bake for about 90 minutes. Allow the cake to cool in the tin for 10 minutes, then transfer it to a cooling rack. Once cool, cut it into three or four layers using a warmed knife.

5. Place all of the ingredients for the mascarpone cream filling in a bowl and mix well. Refrigerate for 30 minutes before using.

6. Spread the filling onto the bottom layer of the cake and place the next layer on top. Continue, spreading the mascarpone cream between each layer.

7. Decorate the top and sides of the cake with the remaining cream and finish with curls or shavings of white and dark chocolate. Serve with single cream.

Fairy Cakes

Fairy Cakes

You will need:
- 225 g (8 oz) self-raising flour
- 80 g (3 oz) margarine
- 80 g (3 oz) caster sugar
- 1 egg
- 75–100 ml (3–4 fl.oz) milk

For the water icing:
- 100 g (4 oz) icing sugar
- 1–2 tablespoons of water
- food colouring

For royal icing:
- 100 g (4 oz) icing sugar
- 1 egg white
- food colouring

Makes 10–12

1. Preheat the oven to 200°C / 400°F / gas mark 6.

2. Put twelve paper cases in a bun case baking tray. Sift the flour into a bowl.

3. Put the margarine in the bowl. Use your fingertips to rub the margarine and flour together until the mixture becomes crumbly.

4. Add the sugar and mix it in, then stir in the egg. Finally, add enough milk to make the mixture creamy.

5. Put spoonfuls of the mixture into the paper cases. Bake the buns for 10–15 minutes, until they are golden brown, then leave them to cool.

Decorating your cakes:
For water icing: Sift the icing sugar into a bowl. Add 1–2 tablespoons of hot water and mix until you have a smooth thick paste.

You can decorate your cakes with sprinkles, balls or sweets. Once the water icing has set, why not pipe decorations with royal icing?

To make royal icing: Beat an egg white in a bowl. Sift the icing sugar into the bowl. Beat the mixture until the icing becomes smooth and thick. Add a drop of food colouring if you wish. Spoon the icing into an icing syringe and carefully pipe your decoration onto the cakes.

Butterfly Buns

Butterfly Buns

You will need:
- 100 g (4 oz) butter
- 100 g (4 oz) granulated sugar
- 2 eggs
- 100 g (4 oz) self-raising flour
- glacé cherries, to decorate

For the buttercream icing:
- 80 g (3 oz) butter
- 150 g (5 oz) icing sugar
- 1–2 tbsp milk
- food colouring (optional)

Makes 12

1. Preheat the oven to 190°C / 375°F / gas mark 5.

2. Put the paper bun cases in the bun tray.

3. Put the butter and sugar into a mixing bowl. Use a wooden spoon to beat them together until the mixture is fluffy and very pale in colour.

4. Beat in the eggs, one at a time, adding a tablespoon of flour with each one.

5. Sift the rest of the flour into the bowl. Use a tablespoon to mix the ingredients gently, as if you were drawing a figure-of-eight. This will make sure your mixture stays nice and fluffy.

6. Use a teaspoon to transfer equal amounts of the mixture to the bun cases. Bake the buns for 20–25 minutes or until they are well risen and golden brown. Leave them to cool on a wire rack.

7. To make the butterfly wings, cut a slice from the top of each cake. Now cut each slice in half.

To make the buttercream icing:

1. Use a wooden spoon or an electric mixer to beat the butter in a large bowl until it is soft.

2. Sift half of the icing sugar into the bowl, and then beat it with the butter until the mixture is smooth. Then sift the rest of the icing sugar into the bowl and add one tablespoon of milk.

3. Beat the mixture until it is smooth and creamy. Now, add a couple of drops of food colouring if you want to.

4. If the mixture is too thick, add a little extra milk to make it more runny. Add extra icing sugar if you need to thicken the mixture.

5. Place a little buttercream icing on top of each bun. Now, gently push two of the halved slices into the icing on each bun at an angle to form pretty butterfly wings. Top with halved glacé cherries to finish.

Raspberry Chocolate Cupcakes

Raspberry Chocolate Cupcakes

You will need:
- 50 g (2 oz) dark chocolate
- 120 ml (4 fl.oz) water
- 100 g (4 oz) butter, softened
- 225 g (8 oz) brown sugar
- 2 eggs
- 100 g (4 oz) self-raising flour
- 2 tbsp cocoa powder
- 50 g (2 oz) ground almonds
- 100 g (4 oz) frozen raspberries

For the topping:
- 150 g (5 oz) butter, softened
- 250 g (9 oz) icing sugar
- a few drops of vanilla essence
- 2 tbsp hot water
- 3 drops of red food colouring
- chocolate sprinkles, to decorate

Makes 10–12

1. Preheat the oven to 180°C / 350°F / gas mark 4.

2. Put the paper cases in the bun tin.

3. Place the chocolate and water into a small saucepan. Stir over a low heat until melted and smooth. Set aside to cool.

4. Place the eggs, sugar and butter in a large mixing bowl. Beat with an electric whisk until just combined.

5. Sift in the flour and cocoa. Add in the ground almonds. Stir well to combine. Add the warm chocolate to the mixture and stir until just combined.

6. Use a teaspoon to transfer equal amounts of the mixture to the paper cases. Place a couple of raspberries in the middle of each one. Bake the cupcakes for about 20–25 minutes. Leave to cool on a wire rack.

7. For the topping, beat together the butter and icing sugar. Once well mixed, add the vanilla essence, food colouring and water. Beat until smooth. Swirl over your cupcakes and decorate with sprinkles.

Carrot Cake

Carrot Cake

You will need:
- 150 g (5 oz) soft brown sugar
- 2 eggs
- 150 g (5 oz) self-raising flour
- 1 tsp baking powder
- 50 g (2 oz) chopped walnuts
- 50 g (2 oz) raisins
- 100 g (4 oz) grated carrots
- 150 ml (5 fl.oz) oil

For the topping:
- 80 g (3 oz) soft cheese
- a few drops of vanilla essence
- 50 g (2 oz) icing sugar

Serves 10–12

1. Preheat the oven to 180°C / 350°F / gas mark 4.

2. Put a cake tin on a sheet of greaseproof paper. Draw around it and cut out the shape. Grease the tin with a little margarine. Put the greaseproof paper inside.

3. Sift the flour and baking powder into a bowl. Add the sugar, nuts, raisins and carrots and stir them together well.

4. Add the eggs and oil to the bowl. Beat all of the ingredients together until they are well mixed.

5. Spoon the mixture into the prepared tin, spreading it into the corners, and smooth the top with a spoon. Bake the cake for one hour, or until it is firm to the touch. Once it has cooled, cut the cake in half with a sharp knife.

6. To make the topping, mix the icing sugar, cream cheese and vanilla essence together.

7. Spread the topping mixture over the top of each cake half. Then, carefully sandwich the two together. Continue to spread the topping around the outside of the cake. Keep the cake in the fridge until you are ready to serve it.

Summer Garden Cupcakes

Summer Garden Cupcakes

You will need:
- 3 eggs
- 150 g (5 oz) butter, softened
- 150 g (5 oz) sugar
- 175 g (6 oz) self-raising flour
- a few drops of vanilla essence
- 2 drops of green food colouring

For the topping:
- 150 g (5 oz) butter, softened
- 250 g (9 oz) icing sugar
- a few drops of vanilla essence
- 2 tsp hot water
- 2 drops of green food colouring

Makes 12–15

1. Preheat the oven to 190°C / 375°F / gas mark 5.

2. Put the paper cases in the bun tin.

3. Crack the eggs into a bowl and beat lightly with a fork.

4. Place the butter, sugar, flour and vanilla into a large bowl. Add the beaten egg and a couple of drops of green food colouring.

5. Beat with an electric mixer for 2 minutes, until the mixture is light and creamy.

6. Use a teaspoon to transfer equal amounts of the mixture to the paper cases. Bake the cupcakes for 18–20 minutes. Leave them to cool on a wire rack.

7. For the topping, beat together the butter and icing sugar. Once well mixed, add the vanilla, food colouring and water. Beat until smooth and creamy. Swirl over your cupcakes and decorate with flowers. If you use real flowers, remember to remove them before eating!

Yummy Cupcakes

Yummy Cupcakes

You will need:
- 225 g (8 oz) self-raising flour
- 80 g (3 oz) margarine
- 80 g (3 oz) caster sugar
- 1 egg
- 80–100 ml (3–4 fl.oz) milk

For the topping:
- freshly whipped cream
- sugar sprinkles

Makes 10–12

1. Preheat the oven to 180°C / 350°F / gas mark 4.

2. Put twelve paper cases in a bun case baking tray. Sift the flour into a bowl.

3. Put the margarine in the bowl. Use the tips of your fingers to rub the margarine and flour together until the mixture becomes crumbly.

4. Add the sugar and mix it in, then stir in the egg. Finally, add enough milk to make the mixture creamy.

5. Put spoonfuls of the mixture into the paper cases. Bake the buns for 10–15 minutes, until they are golden brown, then leave them to cool on a wire rack.

6. Leave the cupcakes in the tray until they are cool, and then decorate them with freshly whipped cream and sugar sprinkles.

Chocolate Fudge Brownies

Chocolate Fudge Brownies

You will need:
- 2 eggs
- 225 g (8 oz) caster sugar
- 100 g (4 oz) butter
- 3 tbsp cocoa powder
- 100 g (4 oz) self-raising flour
- 50 g (2 oz) pecans, chopped

For the fudge icing:
- 50 g (2 oz) butter
- 1 tbsp milk
- 100 g (4 oz) icing sugar
- 2 tbsp cocoa powder
- pecan or walnut halves, to decorate

Makes 15

1. Preheat the oven to 180°C / 350°F / gas mark 4.

2. Beat the eggs and the sugar together in a bowl, until light and fluffy.

3. Melt the butter and beat in the cocoa powder before adding to the eggs and sugar. Sift the flour and fold into the main mix with the pecans.

4. Pour into a lined, greased 20 cm (8 in.) square cake tin. Bake for 40–45 minutes.

To make the fudge icing:

1. Melt the butter and add the milk. Remove from the heat, then beat in the icing sugar and cocoa powder.

2. Spread icing over the cooked brownie and decorate with pecans or walnut halves. Cut into squares when the topping is firm.

Berry and White Chocolate Teatime Muffins

Berry and White Chocolate Teatime Muffins

You will need:

- 200 g (7 oz) self-raising flour
- 100 g (4 oz) caster sugar
- 2 tsp dried coffee granules
- 2 free-range eggs
- 1 tbsp extra virgin olive oil
- 150 ml (5 fl.oz) full cream milk
- 100 g (4 oz) white chocolate, broken into small chunks
- 100 g (4 oz) fresh or frozen mixed forest berries
- 1 grated dessert apple

Makes 9

1. Preheat the oven to 200°C / 400°F / gas mark 6 and grease a muffin tray, unless you are going to use muffin cases.

2. Sift the flour into the sugar and coffee granules in a large mixing bowl, leaving a well in the middle.

3. In a separate bowl, beat together the eggs, oil and milk.

4. Add the egg mixture to the flour and mix it roughly, ignoring any lumps. Then, add the white chocolate chunks, berries and apple.

5. Mix all of the ingredients together roughly. Do not over-mix. Spoon immediately into the muffin tins or muffin cases, so that they are two thirds full.

6. Cook in the centre of the oven for 20–25 minutes. Allow the muffins to cool for 5 minutes before removing them from the tin.

7. Muffins are best enjoyed warm. Any leftover muffins can be reheated for a few minutes in the oven the next day.

Black Cherry Crunchy Filo Flan

Black Cherry Crunchy Filo Flan

You will need:

- 100 g (4 oz) flour
- 15 g (½ oz) sugar
- 80 g (3 oz) butter
- 25 g (1 oz) lard
- 1 egg yolk
- 450 g (1 lb) tinned black cherry pie filling
- 2 sheets of filo pastry
- 25 g (1 oz) melted butter
- 25 g (1 oz) icing sugar
- black cherries, to decorate

Serves 4–6

1. Mix the flour and sugar in a large bowl. Mix in butter and lard lightly to form coarse breadcrumbs.

2. Mix the egg yolk and combine to make a firm dough. Then, cover and refrigerate to rest.

3. Roll the chilled mixture thinly and use to line a 20 cm (8 in.) flan tin with a removable base. Prick the base with a fork, line with silicone paper and fill with baking beans.

4. Leave the edges overhanging until the pastry has rested for 20 minutes and then trim neatly. Bake in a preheated oven for 10–15 minutes at 190°C / 365°F / gas mark 4 until the sides are set but not coloured. Remove the silicone and the baking beans.

5. Half fill the flan with the black cherry pie filling.

6. Snip or cut the filo pastry into jagged small pieces. Gently mix with a little melted butter and turn over to thoroughly coat, scatter thickly over the cherries to completely cover.

7. Return to the oven until the flan is cooked and the filo top is golden and crisp. Cool slightly, dust with icing sugar and top with a couple of cherries to serve.

Lemon Cheesecake with Strawberries and Blueberries

Lemon Cheesecake with Strawberries and Blueberries

You will need:

- 150 g (5 oz) digestive biscuits (crushed)
- 50 g (2 oz) crushed hazelnuts
- 80 g (3 oz) melted butter
- 360 g (12 oz) curd cheese
- 50 g (2 oz) caster sugar
- 3 eggs, separated
- freshly grated zest and juice of 1 lemon
- 15 g (½ oz) gelatine (powdered)
- 300 ml (10 fl.oz) whipping cream
- 225 g (8 oz) strawberries
- 100 g (4 oz) blueberries

Serves 6

1. Mix the digestive biscuits, crushed hazelnuts and melted butter together and spoon into a 20 cm (8 in.) stainless cake ring on a serving plate. Chill until firm.

2. In a bowl, heat the curd cheese with the sugar, egg yolks and lemon zest. Dissolve the gelatine with the lemon juice over heat and stir into the cheese mixture.

3. Fold in the lightly beaten cream. Whisk the egg whites until stiff and fold in.

4. Cut the strawberries in half and stand up around the cake ring, then spoon in the cheesecake mixture and press out to the sides. Level off, cover and chill until set.

5. Arrange half of the strawberries around the top edge and fill the centre with blueberries. When required, slide a sharp knife around the edge and remove the ring.

Baked Blueberry Cheesecake

Baked Blueberry Cheesecake

You will need:
- 150 g (5 oz) crushed digestive biscuits
- 50 g (2 oz) butter (melted)
- 170 g (6 oz) cottage cheese
- 150 g (5 oz) natural yogurt
- 1 tsp plain flour
- 15 g (½ oz) caster sugar
- 1 egg, plus 1 egg white
- juice and grated zest of half a lemon
- 200 g (7 oz) blueberries
- mint leaves, to decorate

Serves 6

1. Grease and line a 20 cm (8 in.) tin. Mix the digestive biscuits and melted butter together and spoon into the tin. Chill until firm.

2. Place the cottage cheese in a food processor and process until smooth.

3. Mix in the yogurt, flour, sugar, egg and egg white. Stir gently, then mix in the lemon zest and juice. Lastly fold in the blueberries, saving a few for decoration.

4. Pour the mixture onto the biscuit base and bake in a preheated oven at 180°C / 350°F / gas mark 4 for 30–35 minutes or until just set. Turn off the oven and leave for another 30 minutes.

5. Run a knife around the cheesecake and carefully turn out onto a serving plate. Decorate with the remaining blueberries and mint leaves to finish.

Raspberry and Chocolate Cheesecake

Raspberry and Chocolate Cheesecake

You will need:
- 250 g (9 oz) digestive biscuits
- 100 g (4 oz) butter, melted
- 450 g (1 lb) soft cream cheese
- 4 free-range eggs
- 1 vanilla pod, seeds scraped out
- 225 g (8 oz) white chocolate
- 225 g (8 oz) crème fraîche
- 100 g (4 oz) raspberries to decorate

For the chocolate sauce:
- 15 g (½ oz) cornflour
- 280 ml (10 fl.oz) milk
- 15 g (½ oz) butter
- 50 g (2 oz) sugar
- 50 g (2 oz) dark chocolate

Serves 8–10

1. Preheat the oven to 150°C / 300°F / gas mark 2.

2. Butter and line a 25 cm (10 in.) loose-bottomed tin with baking parchment. Then, put the biscuits in a plastic food bag and crush using a rolling pin. Transfer the crumbs to a bowl, then pour over the melted butter. Mix thoroughly until the crumbs are completely coated. Tip them into the prepared tin and press firmly down into the base to create an even layer. Chill in the fridge for 1 hour to set firmly.

3. Beat the cream cheese in a bowl until soft, then add the eggs, along with the seeds scraped from the vanilla pod.

4. Melt the white chocolate in a bowl set over a pan of gently simmering water, making sure the bowl doesn't touch the water. Then, fold in the crème fraîche until smooth.

5. Fold the chocolate mixture into the cream cheese mixture. Pour the chocolate and cream cheese mixture into the tin and bang down on a firm surface to remove any air bubbles.

6. Bake in the oven for 45 minutes–1 hour, or until the centre is just firm.

7. Allow to rest for several hours to firm up, before turning out. Decorate the top of the cheesecake with raspberries.

To make the sauce:

1. Mix the cornflour with a little milk.

2. Boil the remaining milk, whisk in the cornflour mixture and add the butter and sugar.

3. Reboil carefully and grate the dark chocolate into the hot (but not boiling) sauce, and whisk until smooth.

4. Pour over the cheesecake and serve.

Chocolate and Almond Fridge Cake

Chocolate and Almond Fridge Cake

You will need:

- 200 g (7 oz) digestive style biscuits
- 150 g (5 oz) dark chocolate
- 100 g (4 oz) milk chocolate
- 50 g (2 oz) unsalted butter
- 50 g (2 oz) honey
- pinch of cinnamon
- pinch of white pepper
- 25 g (1 oz) blanched almonds, roughly chopped
- 50 g (2 oz) candied citrus peel, finely chopped

Serves 8–10

1. Place the biscuits in a strong plastic food bag and crush them roughly with a rolling pin.

2. Break the chocolate into small pieces and melt it in a heatproof bowl over a saucepan of simmering water, stirring occasionally. (Make sure that the bowl is not touching the water.)

3. As soon as the chocolate has melted, add the butter, cut into small dice, honey, cinnamon and pepper. Stir over the heat until well mixed. Off the heat, add the biscuits, almonds and chopped citrus peel and mix thoroughly.

4. Press into a 20 cm (8 in.) greased and lined square tin and allow to cool.

5. Chill in the fridge overnight.

6. While still in the tin, cut the fridge cake into thick fingers. (They are best stored in a container in the fridge.)

7. Remove the cake from the fridge 15 minutes before serving and sprinkle each slice with icing sugar.

Marshmallow Cornflake Drops

Marshmallow Cornflake Drops

You will need:
- 50 g (2 oz) butter
- 225 g (8 oz) marshmallows
- 180 g (6 oz) cornflakes

Makes approximately 25

1. Melt the butter and marshmallows in a pan over a low heat, stirring until melted.

2. Remove from the heat and add the cornflakes, mixing well with a moistened spoon.

3. Shape into small balls and place on silicone paper, until cool and firm.

4. Store in an airtight container.

Kiwi and Toasted Almond Pavlova

Kiwi and Toasted Almond Pavlova

You will need:
- 4 egg whites
- pinch of salt
- 225 g (8 oz) caster sugar
- 1 tsp white vinegar
- 1 tsp cornflour

For the filling:
- 400 ml (14 fl.oz) double cream
- 50 g (2 oz) flaked almonds
- 15 g (½ oz) icing sugar
- 6 kiwi fruit, peeled and sliced

Serves 6

1. Beat the egg whites in a clean bowl with the salt until they form stiff peaks. Gradually beat in the caster sugar until smooth and glossy, then fold in the white vinegar and cornflour.

2. Draw a 23 cm (9 in.) circle on silicone paper and spread the meringue evenly over the circle. Smooth with a palette knife and bake in a preheated oven at 140°C / 275°F / gas mark 1 for 10 minutes. Reduce the heat to 100°C / 225°F, cook for 45 minutes, then turn off.

3. Allow to stand for approximately one hour, then transfer to a serving plate to cool.

To make the filling:

1. Whip the cream and spread half of it over the meringue.

2. Lightly toast the flaked almonds until golden brown, dust with icing sugar and glaze under the grill for a few seconds.

3. Decorate the meringue with the sliced kiwi, remaining double cream and flaked almonds.

Cookies

Coconut Macaroons

Coconut Macaroons

You will need:

- 2 egg whites
- pinch of salt
- 150 g (5 oz) caster sugar
- 150 g (5 oz) desiccated coconut
- rice paper
- 10 glacé cherries, halved

Makes 20

1. Preheat the oven to 160°C / 320°F / gas mark 3.

2. In a bowl, whisk the egg whites with the salt, adding the sugar, a little at a time, until the mixture is stiff and forming peaks. Gently fold in the coconut.

3. Line a baking tray with rice paper and put 20 well spaced spoonfuls of the mixture onto the paper. Top each with half a glacé cherry. Bake for 25–30 minutes until firm.

4. Leave to cool on the rice paper. Tear or cut the paper around each macaroon when cool.

Double Chocolate and Orange Cookies

Double Chocolate and Orange Cookies

You will need:

- 150 g (5 oz) unsalted butter, softened
- 50 g (2 oz) light brown sugar
- 225 g (8 oz) plain flour
- 50 g (2 oz) unsweetened cocoa powder
- 2 tsp baking powder
- 80 g (3 oz) dark chocolate, chopped
- grated zest of 2 oranges
- 2 tbsp orange juice

Makes 30

1. Preheat the oven to 180°C / 350°F / gas mark 4. Line two baking trays with baking parchment.

2. Beat the butter and sugar together in a bowl, until pale and fluffy. Sift the flour, cocoa and baking powder together twice and then carefully fold into the butter and sugar mixture.

3. Add the chopped chocolate, orange zest and orange juice and gently mix together to form a smooth dough.

4. On a lightly-floured surface, roll out the dough to a thickness of ½ cm (¼ in.) Cut into approximately 30 biscuits with a 5 cm (2 in.) fluted biscuit cutter. Cook in the centre of the oven for 12–15 minutes.

5. Allow the biscuits to cool on the baking trays for 5 minutes before transferring them to a wire rack. Store in an airtight container when cold.

Chocolate Chip Cookies

Chocolate Chip Cookies

You will need:

- 80 g (3 oz) butter
- 80 g (3 oz) caster sugar
- 100 g (4 oz) self-raising flour
- 2 tsp cocoa powder
- 80 g (3 oz) chocolate chips
- 100 ml (4 fl.oz) milk

Makes 20

1. Preheat the oven to 180°C / 350°F / gas mark 4.

2. Cream the butter and sugar together in a bowl, until light and fluffy. Sift the flour and cocoa powder into the creamed mixture and stir well.

3. Add two-thirds of the chocolate chips and the milk, mixing in small quantities at a time.

4. Place teaspoons of the cookie dough on a greased baking tray. Sprinkle the remaining chocolate chips on top, and bake in the oven for 15–20 minutes or until golden.

5. Leave to cool for 2 minutes on the tray before lifting onto a wire rack to cool completely.

White Chocolate and Exotic Fruit Cookies

White Chocolate and Exotic Fruit Cookies

You will need:

- 200 g (7 oz) plain flour
- 1 tsp baking powder
- 100 g (4 oz) unsalted butter
- 100 g (4 oz) light brown sugar
- 80 g (3 oz) white chocolate, chopped
- 80 g (3 oz) of mixed exotic dried fruit
  (papaya, pineapple, mango etc) chopped
- 1 tsp lemon zest
- 1 egg

Makes approximately 18

1. Preheat the oven to 190°C / 375°F / gas mark 5. Line two baking trays with lightly greased baking parchment.

2. Sift the flour and baking powder into a bowl. Rub the butter into the flour with your fingertips.

3. Mix in the sugar, chopped chocolate and dried fruit. Add the lemon zest and egg, plus a little extra water if necessary, to form a soft dough.

4. Place spoonfuls of the mixture on the baking trays, pressing each mound down slightly with the back of a spoon. Cook for 10–12 minutes until the cookies are a light, golden brown.

5. Allow to cool for 5 minutes, then transfer to a wire rack. Store in an airtight container.

Gingerbread People

Gingerbread People

You will need:

- 100 g (4 oz) butter
- 80 g (3 oz) brown sugar
- 1 egg yolk
- 1 tsp bicarbonate of soda
- 4 tsp ground ginger
- 360 g (12 oz) flour
- 2 tbsp golden syrup
- 100 g (4 oz) dark chocolate

Makes about 10–15

1. Preheat the oven to 180°C / 350°F / gas mark 4.

2. Cream the butter and sugar together in a bowl until light and fluffy. Carefully work in the egg yolk, then add the sieved bicarbonate of soda, ginger and flour, and mix well.

3. Add the syrup to form a dough; knead until smooth, then divide into five or six pieces.

4. Roll each piece into a ball and sandwich between two sheets of silicone paper. Using a rolling pin, roll over the top of the sheets to form an even layer approximately 1 cm (½ in.) thick. Carefully remove the top sheet of paper and place the bottom sheet on a baking tray.

5. Use a gingerbread person cutter to cut out the biscuit, then carefully peel away the waste from the dough leaving the people shapes on the paper. Bake for 10–12 minutes then slide onto a wire rack to cool.

6. Meanwhile, melt the chocolate over a pan of hot water. Dip the legs and heads into the chocolate for shoes and hair, and leave on silicone paper to set. Use the remaining chocolate in a piping bag to add the smaller features, such as eyes, buttons and belts, then leave to set completely.

Colourful Cookies

You will need:
- 100 g (4 oz) butter
- 100 g (4 oz) caster sugar
- 1 egg
- 225 g (8 oz) plain flour
- assorted sweets

For the royal icing:
- 1 egg white
- 100 g (4 oz) icing sugar
- various food colourings

For the water icing:
- 100 g (4 oz) icing sugar
- 1–2 tbsp water
- various food colourings

Makes 20–30

1. Preheat the oven to 180°C / 350°F / gas mark 4.

2. Cream the butter and sugar together in a bowl, until light and fluffy. Add the egg and mix well.

3. Sift the flour into the creamed mixture and, using your hands, create a smooth, firm dough. Refrigerate the mixture for 15 minutes.

4. Roll the dough out on a floured surface until 5 mm thick. Using either a sharp knife or cutters, cut out various shapes and transfer to a greased baking tray. Bake in the oven for 10 minutes or until golden brown.

5. Cool the cookies on wire racks.

To make the royal icing:
Lightly beat the egg white. Add the sieved icing sugar and beat until the mixture thickens. Separate into different bowls and add various food colourings as desired. Transfer to a piping tool or bag to decorate the biscuits.

To make the water icing:
Add enough water to the icing sugar to make a thick, smooth paste. Spread the water icing over the cookies with a palette knife or spoon, then pipe the royal icing on for finer details. Decorate with additional sweets if desired.

Oat Crunch Cookies

Oat Crunch Cookies

You will need:
- 100 g (4 oz) butter
- 80 g (3 oz) demerara sugar
- 100 g (4 oz) plain wholemeal flour
- 100 g (4 oz) porridge oats

Makes approximately 25

1. Preheat the oven to 180°C / 350°F / gas mark 4.

2. Cream the butter and sugar together in a bowl, until light. Add the flour and oats to the mixture and use your hands to create a soft dough.

3. Roll the dough out on a floured surface until 5 mm thick and cut into 25 rounds with a 5 cm (2 in.) cutter. Bake in the oven for 12–15 minutes or until cooked.

4. Transfer to a wire rack to cool. Store in an airtight container.

Honey Flapjacks with Pecans and Almonds

Honey Flapjacks with Pecans and Almonds

You will need:

- 200 g (7 oz) butter
- 3 tbsp clear honey
- 200 g (7 oz) demerara sugar
- 285 g (9½ oz) jumbo rolled oats
- 100 g (4 oz) desiccated coconut
- 50 g (2 oz) flaked almonds
- 50 g (2 oz) pecans, lightly crushed

Makes 25–30

1. Preheat the oven to 180°C / 350°F / gas mark 4.

2. Gently heat the butter, honey and demerara sugar in a large saucepan until just melted.

3. Stir in the oats, coconut, flaked almonds and pecan nuts, and mix well.

4. Spread the mixture evenly in a well oiled 20 cm (8 in.) square baking tray. Bake in the oven for approximately 30 minutes.

5. Allow to cool in the tray for 10–12 minutes, then cut into squares with a sharp knife. Transfer the flapjacks to a wire rack to cool completely. Store in an airtight container.

Almond Maraschino Biscuits

You will need:

- 25 g (1 oz) nibbed almonds
- 100 g (4 oz) plain flour
- 25 g (1 oz) ground almonds
- 50 g (2 oz) caster sugar
- 50 g (2 oz) butter
- 1 egg yolk
- 2 tsps maraschino liqueur

For the maraschino icing:

- 80 g (3 oz) icing sugar
- 1 tbsp maraschino liqueur
- 2 tbsp hot water

Makes approximately 25

1. Preheat the oven to 180°C / 350°F / gas mark 4.

2. Toast the nibbed almonds until golden brown.

3. Mix the sieved flour, ground almonds and sugar in a large bowl and rub in the butter until the mixture resembles fine breadcrumbs.

4. Add the egg yolk and maraschino liqueur and mix together to form a dough.

5. Allow to rest for 10 minutes, then roll out on a lightly floured surface until approximately 4 mm thick. Cut into rounds using a 6 cm (2½ in.) fluted cutter and place on baking sheets lined with silicone paper.

6. Bake for 10–12 minutes or until pale, golden brown. Allow to cool on wire racks.

To make the maraschino icing:

Sift the icing sugar into a clean bowl, add the maraschino liqueur and hot water, and stir until smooth, adding more water if required. Spoon a little icing into the centre of each biscuit and smooth out to the edges. Sprinkle the toasted nibbed almonds on top.

Coffee and Hazelnut Biscotti

Coffee and Hazelnut Biscotti

You will need:

- 100 g (4 oz) caster sugar
- 1 beaten egg
- 100 g (4 oz) plain flour
- 1 tbsp instant coffee
- ½ tsp vanilla essence
- ½ tbsp baking powder
- 100 g (4 oz) hazelnuts, toasted and chopped roughly
- 100 g (4 oz) white chocolate

Makes approximately 20

1. Preheat the oven to 180°C / 350°F / gas mark 4.

2. Beat the sugar and egg together in a bowl and stir in the sieved flour, coffee, vanilla essence, baking powder and nuts to form a dough.

3. Roll into a small, slightly flattened, loaf shape and bake for approximately 25 minutes covered with foil. Remove the foil and allow to stand until cool.

4. Reduce the oven temperature to 160°C / 320°F / gas mark 3.

5. Use a very sharp, serrated knife to cut thin slices diagonally. Place on baking sheets lined with silicone paper. Bake for a further 10–15 minutes until crisp, turning halfway.

6. Cool on wire racks.

7. Meanwhile, melt the white chocolate in a bowl over a pan of hot water. When the biscotti have cooled, carefully cover one side of each cookie with chocolate and leave to set.

Orange, Lemon and Lime Crunchies

Orange, Lemon and Lime Crunchies

You will need:

- 100 g (4 oz) butter
- 80 g (3 oz) caster sugar
- grated rind of ½ orange
- juice and zest of ½ lemon
- 1 tsp lime juice
- 50 g (2 oz) ground walnuts
- 150 g (5 oz) self-raising flour
- 25 g (1 oz) crushed walnuts

Makes 30

1. Preheat the oven to 190°C / 375°F / gas mark 5.

2. Cream the butter and 50 g (2 oz) of the sugar in a bowl, then add the orange rind, lemon juice and zest, lime juice and ground walnuts.

3. Beat in the sieved flour until the mixture begins to hold together.

4. Divide the dough into 30 small balls. Drop each one into the crushed walnuts and remaining sugar. Flatten each ball slightly and place on greased silicone paper on a baking tray. Bake for 10–12 minutes, until golden.

5. Allow to cool, then transfer to wire racks. Store in an airtight container.

Traditional Shortbread

Traditional Shortbread

You will need:

- 240 g (8 oz) butter
- 300 g (10 oz) plain flour
- 2 tbsp ground rice
- 50 g (2 oz) icing sugar

Makes 24 biscuits or 2 'wheels' of shortbread

1. Preheat the oven to 160°C / 320°F / gas mark 3.

2. Rub the butter into the sieved flour, ground rice and icing sugar.

3. Bring the dough together and press into two greased, 17 cm (7 in.) cake tins. Use your finger to crimp around the edges and prick the surface with a fork to prevent the mixture rising. Score the surface of each wheel into 12 segments with the back of a knife.

4. Bake in the oven for 35–40 minutes, until a pale golden brown. Leave to stand in the tins for 10–15 minutes, then lift out onto a wire rack to cool. Store in an airtight container.

Note: *This mixture can also be used to press into the traditional carved, wooden mould which produces ornately patterned shortbread biscuits.*

Crunchy Apricot Sticks

Crunchy Apricot Sticks

You will need:

- 100 g (4 oz) butter
- 100 g (4 oz) brown sugar
- a few drops of vanilla essence
- 1 egg
- 80 g (3 oz) self-raising flour
- ½ tsp salt
- 80 g (3 oz) wheatgerm
- 50 g (2 oz) desiccated coconut
- 50 g (2 oz) rolled oats
- 100 g (4 oz) dried apricots, chopped
- 50 g (2 oz) cornflakes
- 100 g (4 oz) dark chocolate

Makes approximately 25

1. Preheat the oven to 180°C / 350°F / gas mark 4.

2. Cream the butter, brown sugar, vanilla essence and egg together in a bowl.

3. Stir in the flour, salt, wheatgerm, coconut, rolled oats, chopped apricots and cornflakes and mix well.

4. Take one tablespoon of mixture, roll it gently in your hands to form a finger and place on a baking sheet lined with silicone paper. Flatten slightly to firm. Repeat with the rest of the mixture and bake for 10–12 minutes.

5. Leave to cool on wire racks.

6. Meanwhile, melt the chocolate in a bowl over a pan of boiling water.

7. Dip the bases into the melted chocolate and drizzle some chocolate over the biscuits.

Apricot and Pistachio Biscuits

Apricot and Pistachio Biscuits

You will need:

- 50 g (2 oz) almond marzipan
- 80 g (3 oz) butter
- 2 tsp grated lime zest
- 1 tbsp lime juice
- 50 g (2 oz) caster sugar
- 1 egg, separated
- 150 g (5 oz) plain flour
- 1 tsp water
- 50 g (2 oz) flaked almonds
- 25 g (1 oz) chopped pistachio nuts
- 50 g (2 oz) apricot jam

Makes approximately 25

1. Preheat the oven to 180°C / 350°F / gas mark 4.

2. Combine the marzipan, butter, lime zest and juice, sugar and egg yolk in a large bowl.

3. Sift the flour into the mixture and knead gently until firm. Refrigerate for 20–30 minutes.

4. Roll the dough out on a floured surface until it is 1 cm (½ in.) thick, then cut into rounds with a 5 cm (2 in.) fluted cutter. Place on a baking sheet lined with silicone paper.

5. Mix the egg white and water together and brush over the top of the biscuits before sprinkling with flaked almonds and chopped pistachios.

6. Bake for 10–15 minutes until pale golden brown.

7. Leave to cool, then brush with sieved apricot jam and return to the oven to glaze for 2–3 minutes. When cold, store in an airtight container.

Chocolate and Coconut Wheatie Crunch

You will need:
- 100 g (4 oz) butter
- 100 g (4 oz) brown sugar
- 1 egg
- 25 g (1 oz) wheatgerm
- 50 g (2 oz) desiccated coconut
- 100 g (4 oz) plain flour
- 50 g (2 oz) self-raising flour
- 100 g (4 oz) plain chocolate

Makes 25–30

1. Preheat the oven to 180°C / 350°F / gas mark 4.

2. Cream the butter and sugar together in a bowl. Beat in the egg, then gently fold in the wheatgerm, coconut and flours. Mix well.

3. Form balls using heaped teaspoons of mixture rolled between your palms, then place on silicone paper. Use the back of a knife blade to slightly flatten the balls, then bake for 10 minutes or until golden and crisp.

4. Transfer to wire racks to cool.

5. Meanwhile, melt the chocolate over a pan of simmering water, and dip the cooled biscuits halfway into the chocolate. Allow to set on a cooling rack. Store in an airtight container when the chocolate has completely set.

Hazelnut and Sesame Fingers

Hazelnut and Sesame Fingers

You will need:
- 180 g (6 oz) ground hazelnuts
- 50 g (2 oz) ground almonds
- 100 g (4 oz) sesame seeds
- 50 g (2 oz) plain flour
- 3 egg whites
- 180 g (6 oz) caster sugar
- 180 g (6 oz) dark chocolate

Makes 25–30

1. Preheat the oven to 160°C / 325°F / gas mark 3.

2. Combine the hazelnuts, almonds, sesame seeds and sieved flour in a bowl and mix well.

3. Place the egg whites in a clean bowl and beat with an electric mixer until stiff. Add sugar and beat until really stiff and velvety.

4. Fold in the nut mixture, then transfer into a piping tool or bag with a large plain tube or nozzle. Pipe fingers of the mixture onto lightly greased silicone paper on baking trays and bake for 12–15 minutes until crisp and golden. Leave to cool.

5. Melt the chocolate in a bowl over a pan of simmering water, then dip in one end of each biscuit. Allow the chocolate on the biscuits to set. Store the biscuits in an airtight container.

Pecan and Coffee Squares

Pecan and Coffee Squares

You will need:
- 100 g (4 oz) butter
- 50 g (2 oz) caster sugar
- 150 g (5 oz) plain flour
- 50 g (2 oz) self-raising flour

For the filling:
- 400 g (14 oz) tinned condensed milk
- 2 tbsp golden syrup
- 25 g (1 oz) butter
- 3 tsp instant coffee granules
- 80 g (3 oz) crushed pecan nuts

For the topping:
- 150 g (5 oz) plain flour
- 1 tsp cinnamon
- 1 tsp instant coffee powder
- 50 g (2 oz) brown sugar
- 100 g (4 oz) butter

Makes 28

1. Preheat the oven to 180°C / 350°F / gas mark 4.

2. Cream the butter and sugar in a bowl.

3. Add the flours to make a firm dough. Press into the base of a well-greased 25–30 cm (10–12 in.) swiss roll tin and bake for 10–12 minutes.

To make the filling:

1. Mix the condensed milk, golden syrup and butter together in a non-stick saucepan.

2. Add the coffee granules, then heat the mixture over a medium heat until it starts to bubble. Stir briskly until it thickens, but do not allow to burn. Mix in the pecans.

To make the topping:

1. Sift the dry ingredients into a bowl and rub in the butter to make a firm dough. Chill in the refrigerator until very firm.

2. Spread the filling over the biscuit base, then coarsely grate the topping over the top. Return to the oven and cook for a further 10–12 minutes, or until firm to the touch. Allow to cool before cutting into squares.

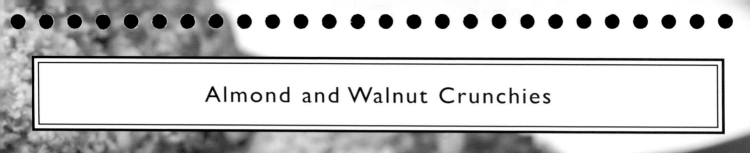

Almond and Walnut Crunchies

Almond and Walnut Crunchies

You will need:

- 180 g (6 oz) blanched almonds
- 2 egg whites
- 100 g (4 oz) caster sugar
- 1 tsp finely grated orange zest
- 2 tbsp orange liqueur
- 50 g (2 oz) crushed walnuts
- 26 walnut halves

Makes 26

1. Preheat the oven to 190°C / 375°F / gas mark 5.

2. Finely chop the blanched almonds in a food processor.

3. Add one egg white, sugar, orange zest and orange liqueur to the almonds and mix until combined.

4. Roll out the dough on a lightly floured surface until it is approximately 1 cm (½ in.) thick, then cut out 26 biscuits using a 5 cm (2 in.) cutter. Place the biscuits on a greased baking sheet.

5. Toast the crushed walnuts in the oven for 3–4 minutes, then finely crush them with a rolling pin. Brush the tops of the biscuits with unbeaten egg white and press into the crushed walnuts. Dip the walnut halves into the egg white and press them into the centre of each biscuit.

6. Bake for 5–10 minutes until golden. Cool on wire racks and store in an airtight container.

Cereal Crisps

Cereal Crisps

You will need:

- 100 g (4 oz) butter
- 180 g (6 oz) caster sugar
- 1 egg
- 100 g (4 oz) self-raising flour
- 25 g (1 oz) plain flour
- 50 g (2 oz) rolled oats
- 50 g (2 oz) sesame seeds
- 50 g (2 oz) flaked almonds, lightly crushed
- 50 g (2 oz) cornflakes

Makes 25–30

1. Preheat the oven to 180°C / 350°F / gas mark 4.

2. Cream the butter and sugar until light and fluffy in a bowl. Beat the egg, and then add it to the mixture.

3. Fold in the flours, oats, seeds, nuts and cornflakes, and mix well.

4. Place tablespoons of the mixture onto lightly oiled silicone paper on a baking tray; press flat and bake for 15 minutes or until golden and crisp.

5. Store in an airtight container.

Hazelnut and Pink Grapefruit Cookies

Hazelnut and Pink Grapefruit Cookies

You will need:
- 150 g (5 oz) plain flour
- 2 tbsp sugar
- 80 g (3 oz) ground hazelnuts
- 100 g (4 oz) butter
- 1 egg yolk
- 1 tsp grated pink grapefruit zest
- 1½ tbsp pink grapefruit juice
- 50 ml (1½ fl.oz) double cream, whipped, to decorate
- 30 whole hazelnuts, to decorate
- orange zest, to decorate

For the filling:
- 50 g (2 oz) butter
- 100 g (4 oz) sugar
- 2 tsp grated, grapefruit zest
- 2 tbsp grapefruit juice
- 2 eggs

Makes 30

1. Preheat the oven to 180°C / 350°F / gas mark 4.

2. Sift the flour and mix with the sugar and hazelnuts.

3. Rub in the butter and add the egg yolk, pink grapefruit zest and juice, mixing to form a smooth dough.

4. Divide the dough into two, press one half into a lined and greased baking tin, approximately 15 x 30 cm (6 x 12 in.) and 1 cm (½ in.) deep. Refrigerate both whilst preparing the filling.

5. Begin the filling by creaming the butter and sugar. Beat in the pink grapefruit zest and juice and then the eggs. The mixture will appear curdled, but this is normal.

6. Spread this mixture over the refrigerated base, and, using the coarse side of a grater, grate the remaining half of the dough over the mixture.

7. Bake for about 30 minutes or until pale, golden brown. Cool on wire racks (during cooling the layers often merge together). Cut into fingers once completely cold.

8. Decorate by piping a noisette of whipped cream in the centre of each cookie and top with hazelnuts and strands of orange zest.

Lemon and Coconut Biscuits

Lemon and Coconut Biscuits

You will need:
- 100 g (4 oz) butter
- 80 g (3 oz) icing sugar
- 1 tsp lemon juice
- 150 g (5 oz) self-raising flour
- 80 g (3 oz) cornflour
- 2 tsp grated lemon zest
- 1 egg yolk
- 2 tsp milk
- extra icing sugar

For the filling:
- 50 g (2 oz) cream cheese
- 2 tbsp cottage cheese
- 2 tbsp sugar
- ½ tsp grated lemon zest
- 1 tbsp coconut flavoured rum
- 2 tbsp desiccated coconut
- 1 egg yolk

Makes 25–30

1. Preheat the oven to 180°C / 350°F / gas mark 4.

2. Cream the butter, icing sugar and lemon juice in a bowl until light and fluffy.

3. Add the flours and lemon zest and mix to form a dough. Knead the dough until smooth, wrap in cling film and refrigerate until firm.

4. Roll out the dough on a floured surface until it is about 3 mm thick. Use a fluted cutter to cut into 6 cm (2½ in.) rounds. Place half of the biscuits on greased silicone paper and brush the edges with a little egg yolk.

To make the filling:
1. Beat the cream cheese, cottage cheese, sugar, lemon zest, coconut flavoured rum and coconut together in a bowl. Mix in the egg yolk and store the mixture in the fridge for 20 minutes.

2. Place half a teaspoon of filling in the centre of each biscuit and place another biscuit on top. Gently press together to seal the edges. Brush the tops with egg wash, made from the remaining egg yolk and a little milk.

3. Bake for 12–15 minutes, until golden brown. Cool on wire racks then dust with icing sugar. Store in an airtight container.

Peanut Crunchies

Peanut Crunchies

You will need:

- 100 g (4 oz) butter
- 50 g (2 oz) caster sugar
- 50 g (2 oz) demerara sugar
- pinch of salt
- ½ tsp vanilla essence
- 80 g (3 oz) peanut butter
- ½ tsp grated lemon zest
- 1 tsp bicarbonate of soda
- 25 g (1 oz) crushed peanuts
- 180 g (6 oz) plain flour

Makes 25–30

1. Preheat the oven to 180°C / 350°F / gas mark 4.

2. Cream the butter, sugars and salt together in a bowl.

3. Beat in the vanilla essence, peanut butter and grated lemon zest.

4. Fold in the bicarbonate of soda, crushed peanuts and the flour, to form a stiff dough. Roll the dough into small balls and place on greased baking sheets.

5. Use a knife to press down the biscuits and bake for 12–15 minutes until crisp and golden. When cold, store in an airtight container.

Chocolate Chip and Peanut Butter Cookies

Chocolate Chip and Peanut Butter Cookies

You will need:

- 135 g (4½ oz) unsalted butter, softened
- 50 g (2 oz) smooth peanut butter
- 80 g (3 oz) sugar
- 2 large eggs
- a few drops of vanilla essence
- 200 g (7 oz) plain flour
- 1 tsp baking powder
- 80 g (3 oz) dark chocolate, chopped
- 50 g (2 oz) unsalted peanuts

Makes approximately 18

1. Preheat the oven to 180°C / 350°F / gas mark 4.

2. Line a baking tray with silicone paper.

3. Beat the butter, peanut butter and sugar in a bowl, until fluffy. Add the beaten eggs and vanilla essence, and mix well.

4. Sift the flour and baking powder together and fold them into the mixture. Add the chopped chocolate and peanuts. Mix in 1–2 tablespoonfuls of milk if the dough appears too stiff.

5. Place evenly spaced spoonfuls of the mixture onto the baking tray, pressing each one down with the back of the spoon. (Dipping the spoon in water will stop it from sticking to the dough.)

6. Bake cookies in the centre of the oven for 20 minutes. Allow them to cool on a wire rack. Store in an airtight container.

Brandy Snap Baskets

Brandy Snap Baskets

You will need:
- 50 g (2 oz) golden syrup
- 50 g (2 oz) caster sugar
- 50 g (2 oz) butter
- 50 g (2 oz) flour
- ½ tsp ground ginger
- grated zest of half a lemon
- 1 tsp brandy

For the filling:
- 425 g (15 oz) tinned black cherries
- 300 ml (10 fl.oz) double cream
- 25 g (1 oz) icing sugar
- 2 tbsp cherry brandy
- fresh mint leaves, to decorate

Serves 6

1. Melt the golden syrup, caster sugar and butter. Mix in the flour, ginger, lemon zest and brandy.

2. Preheat the oven to 180°C / 350°F / gas mark 4. Spoon the mixture into walnut-sized pieces and place onto silicone paper, two at a time. Press to spread, and bake for 8–10 minutes until golden.

3. Leave to cool for a few moments, then drape each one over an individual pudding basin or small cup. Allow to cool.

To make the filling:

1. Chop or liquidise one third of the black cherries. Beat the double cream to soft peaks, fold in the icing sugar, cherry brandy and the puréed black cherries.

2. Continue to beat until stiff. To serve, spoon into the brandy snap baskets and top with the whole cherries. Add a mint leaf to decorate.